P9-CLO-619

Decking the Halls

© 2000 Linda Allen

Illustrations © Patricia Bickner Linder

Published by Willow Creek Press
P.O. Box 147
Minocqua, Wisconsin 54548

All rights reserved. No part of this book may be reproduced or transmitted in
any form by any means, electronic or mechanical, including photocopying,
recording, or by any information storage and retrieval system, without written
permission from the Publisher.

For information on other Willow Creek titles, call 1-800-850-9453.

Library of Congress Cataloging-in-Publication Data
Allen, Linda
Decking the Halls : myths and traditions of Christmas plants / Linda Allen.
p. cm.
ISBN 1-57223-383-4 (hardcover : alk. paper)
1. Christmas trees. 2. Plants--Folklore. 3. Poinsettias.
4. Mistletoes. 5. Christmas decorations. I. Title.
GT4989 .A47 2000
394.2663--DC21
00-009071

Printed in Canada

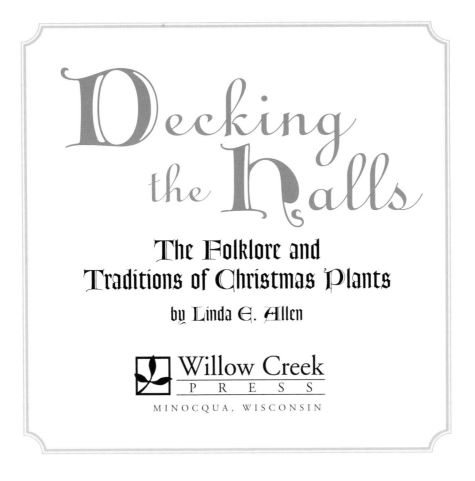

Decking the Halls

The Folklore and Traditions of Christmas Plants

by Linda E. Allen

Willow Creek
P R E S S

MINOCQUA, WISCONSIN

Dedication

The Hanging of the Greens, the annual service that inaugurates the Christmas or Advent season in many churches, is a celebration of ancient traditions blended with modern customs, music, and liturgy. Holly, cedar, evergreens, and the Advent wreath are the plants that provide symbolism and meaning to the service, the inspiration for this book. For this inspiration, I gratefully dedicate *Decking the Halls: Folklore and Traditions of Christmas Plants* to First United Methodist Church, Stillwater, Oklahoma.

Table of Contents

Introduction

Mistletoe Myths

myth *(mith) n. [LL. mythos, < Gr. mythos, a word, speech, story, legend] 1. a traditional story of unknown authorship, ostensibly with a historical basis, but serving usually to explain some phenomenon of nature, the origin of man, or the customs, institutions, religious rites, etc. of a people; myths usually involve the exploits of gods and heroes; cf. LEGEND 2. such stories collectively; mythology 3. any fictitious story, or unscientific account, theory belief, etc. 4. any imaginary person or thing spoken of as though existing*

Because there are so many customs and traditions during the Christmas season, many times we do not pause to wonder and ponder about how and why they began. The reason for the season is unexplainable by science or technology, and many customs and traditions of the season are surrounded by an aura of mystery and magic. Through the years, myths and folklore have blended with traditions to create our modern-day Christmas season. *Decking the Halls* considers the role of many of our popular Christmas plants and flowers on this most holy night.

A Cosmic Christmas Through the Ages

Once upon a time, long, long ago, on a magical, mystical night, the world changed. The magic of the Magi and the mysteries of the mystics could not compare with the wonder of that night. It was a night when legends tell us that stars fell from the sky to become the flowers that we know as buttercups encircling the manger in a glow of golden color, a night when ordinary weeds became majestic, brilliant flowers to honor the Son of God, and a night when animals spoke. It was a simpler time, when science and technology did not explain away the magic and mystery of the unknown, when faith and belief in the incredible were all that were needed in the face of the unexplainable.

We decorate our homes, yards, streets and businesses with lights, candles, greenery accented with red, Santa Claus, and ornaments in all shapes, sizes and colors. We honor our friends and families with special gifts for the season. But why do we do these things year after year? Of course, the obvious reason for Christians is to celebrate the birth of the Christ Child. But many of our seasonal traditions and customs have been borrowed from ancient cultures and practices that existed before the birth of Christ, thus making modern-day Christmas a truly multicultural celebration that unites all mankind in a cosmic celebration. Could this possibly be the real meaning of the Nativity experience?

Of all the seasonal celebrations of the year, Christmas has more traditional plants with their accompanying legends and symbolism than any other season. Holly, ivy, mistletoe, the poinsettia, and the most popular and recognized of all – the Christmas tree – all share the color green symbolizing eternal life. Ancient cultures believed that bringing greenery into the home was a lucky charm that would guarantee the return of vegetation and growth in the spring. Some people even went so far as to adorn themselves with sprigs of greenery to further attract personal luck and good fortune. There were superstitions governing when to bring the greenery into the house. For example, it was considered unlucky to bring greenery into the house before Christmas Eve, and it was equally unlucky to remove it before the Twelfth Night, or January sixth.

Many of our Christmas traditions involving plants come from the ancient Druids, Celts, Norse, and Roman civilizations, all of which worshipped many nature gods. These cultures celebrated a mid-winter holiday known as Saturnalia. This holiday was celebrated in observance of the winter solstice, usually around December 21, the shortest day of the year. Ancient cultures believed that as the sun gradually sank lower into the horizon during the autumn season, it would not return.

In order to entice the sun god to provide warmth, light, and an abundance of crops, they created annual rituals and celebrations. These celebrations of the winter solstice, often wild and riotous, were held to thank the gods for returning the sun to them. The winter solstice restored faith in the future as the days became longer.

Greenery played a special role in these festivities because the green color represented eternal life, coming from plants that remained green throughout the year. Greenery was also used as protection against witches and other evil demons believed to be present, and especially active and powerful, during this time of the year.

As pagan cultures gradually converted to Christianity, the plants involved in the former pagan celebrations began to take on new meanings, and new stories and legends were created to give them Christian significance. Because many plants were alleged to possess supernatural powers of healing, divination, and warding off evil spirits and forces, it was quite natural to dedicate them to the Holy Family as Christianity spread throughout Europe and then to the Americas.

Many folk legends depict Christmas as a magical time when all of nature celebrated wondrous events. Animals spoke and plants that had never bloomed produced glorious and profuse blossoms in honor of Christ's birth. The poinsettia and the Christmas rose were no more than weeds until the Nativity transformed them into beautiful flowers. Even the straw in the manger was said to have burst into glorious golden flowers when Jesus was born. Stars fell from the heavens and planted themselves around the manger as buttercups to honor this special birth. After the Wise Men arrived in Bethlehem, the star that had guided their journey exploded into thousands of fragments and became the flower we now know as the Star of Bethlehem. There is even a legend that all the trees in the forest bloomed and bore fruit on the night of Christ's birth.

Today, understanding the varied cultural histories behind our use of traditional Christmas plants and flowers can inspire unity as we celebrate this most holy season. Perhaps the stories of the miracles of spontaneous blossoms from previously barren plants and weeds turning into glorious flowers will provide additional magic and mystery to an already mystical season.

Much Ado about the Much-Maligned Mistletoe

*I saw Mommy kissing Santa Claus
Underneath the mistletoe last night . . .*

From superstitious to sacred, and from ancient pagans to prairie pioneers, the strange mistletoe plant has carried with it a mysterious history of both aversion and curiosity. Mistletoe has piqued the curiosity and imagination of both saints and sinners for centuries. But how and why did this flower change from a pagan symbol to one of honor and pride for early settlers, and later become the state flower of Oklahoma?

Mistletoe is a rather strange, but beautiful plant with pearly white berries and velvety, green leaves. Although tradition attributes fertility to this plant, it is a parasite that grows on other trees, gaining its beauty and strength from its host tree. Its glossy, white berries are poisonous.

Much of the history of the mistletoe's use comes from the Anglo-Saxons and Druids of northern Europe. Its name comes from the Anglo-Saxon word "misteltan" which means "little dung twig." It was named this because of the role that birds play in its propagation. Birds are attracted to the white, pearly berries for food, dining on them in one place and later excreting them in another, thus propagating the plant randomly over a broad area. Some legends claim that mistletoe will not sprout unless ripened in the bird's stomach.

Mistletoe was sacred to the Druids, the Ainos, and

some African tribes. Because it attaches itself to the upper parts of trees and does not have roots in the ground, it seemed to be a divine gift from the gods just dropped from the heavens. Since the mistletoe was green when all else had "died," it came to symbolize eternal life of the soul because the "soul" of the tree was still "living."

The Druids were forest worshipers who believed the mistletoe had great powers to heal many kinds of illnesses, and that it helped predict the future. They attributed many powers to the mistletoe. It was used as an aphrodisiac that contained powers of fertility; it provided protection from witchcraft and nightmares; it had the ability to open all locks; it protected the stable and dairy from trolls; it was thought to be a cure for epilepsy; it offered protection from death in battle; and, it was used as a divining rod to locate gold or treasure.

Each year, the Druids celebrated the winter solstice with sacred rites involving the mistletoe. They gathered in the woods for the ritual, which was performed by the Arch Druid assisted by his high priests. Because mistletoe growing on an oak tree was considered extremely rare, the Druids regarded mistletoe from the oak with special reverence. The oak tree with the most mistletoe was chosen for the sacred ceremony. The Arch Druid, dressed totally in white, climbed to the branches loaded with mistletoe. He then severed the mistletoe from the tree using a golden sickle, being careful that the mistletoe did not touch the ground. Some versions of the legend say that the Arch Druid caught the mistletoe in his flowing, white robes, while other versions claim that virgins caught it in a white cloth. The Druids then divided the mistletoe among themselves as a symbol of peace and prosperity. They hung it over their doors to ward off evil spirits, to ensure fertility, and to encourage enemies to bury past grudges. They expected guests to embrace under the mistletoe.

The tradition of kissing under the mistletoe dates back to the Roman era when enemies reconciled under the mistletoe. Both Roman and Norse mythology share a story about a mother and son who experienced the mischief, mystery and magic of the mistletoe. In both stories, the plot is the same but the characters are different. In the Roman version, the story involves Venus, the goddess of light, and her son, Apollo, the god of music, poetry, prophecy and medicine. The Norse story's characters include Frigga, the goddess of love, and her son, Balder, the god of light. Venus and Frigga had protected their sons from all dangers in the world except the mistletoe. A sharpened sprig of mistletoe pierced each son's heart as part of a trick by mischievous gods or evil spirits. When the mothers learned of their sons' deaths, their tears of sorrow and grief became the white berries of the mistletoe. When both sons were later brought back to life, Venus and Frigga were so overjoyed that they kissed anyone who walked under the mistletoe.

There is a proper etiquette dating back to ancient times about kissing under the mistletoe: the gentleman should pluck one white berry while kissing the lady on the cheek. One kiss is allowed for each berry. When the last berry is gone, there should be no further kissing. A successful kiss under the mistletoe is said to result in marriage, but girls who refuse to be kissed under the mistletoe will become "old maids." Mistletoe is often burned on the Twelfth Night, or January sixth, to break any superstitions that all who kissed under the mistletoe might never marry.

Because of its association with the Druids and the Romans, mistletoe was never used as a Christmas decoration in the church. A medieval legend also claims that the wood used to make the crucifixion cross was from the mistletoe which, according to this legend, was once a tree. As a punishment for its role in the death of Christ, it was cursed and no longer welcome on earth. The only way it could return was as a parasite dependent on other trees for its survival.

In the not-so-distant past, the mistletoe regained its pride and dignity and became a symbol of endurance and survival to early pioneers and settlers in Oklahoma territory. After Indian Territory was opened for settlement in 1889, the pioneers observed mistletoe in full bloom during their first Christmas. It was growing "as thick as Spanish moss" in the trees along the creeks and river bottoms. A beautiful sight to their work-worn eyes, the mistletoe became an inspiration for settlers, symbolizing survival, hardiness and endurance. In the winter, it was often the only greenery available to put on the graves of loved ones or to decorate weddings. The pioneers were unaffected by its pagan history and reputation.

Because of its inspiration and importance to the early pioneers, an early settler proposed the mistletoe be the official territorial flower to the legislature in 1893. Although some churches protested because of its association with pagans, and some legislators considered the request frivolous, the mistletoe nevertheless became the official flower of the Oklahoma Territory and, later, of the State of Oklahoma. The meaning given to the mistletoe in the language of flowers is "I surmount all difficulties." For the pioneers, the mistletoe truly became an appropriate symbol of endurance in overcoming difficulties and obstacles as they settled a new land.

During a modern Christmas, kissing under the mistletoe has become a popular tradition. Song lyrics refer to the custom too: *I saw Mommy kissing Santa Claus, underneath the mistletoe last night.* This contemporary Christmas decoration often provides the opportunity to express affection or to kiss someone we may not have had the courage to without this ancient symbol. That alone is worth an homage to our many ancestors.

O Christmas Tree

O Tannebaum, O Tannebaum,
Wie treu sind deine Blätter!
O Christmas tree, O Christmas tree,
How faithful are thy leaves!

Probably the most recognized plant decoration during the Christmas season is the Christmas tree. Firs, pines, cedars . . . all make up the group of plants we call evergreens, so named because they retain their green color throughout the year. The word evergreen comes from two Old English words: "aefie" meaning "always," and "gowan," meaning "to grow." The Old Norse word "tre" provides us with our word for tree.

One legend claims the fir was the original "Tree of Life" in the Garden of Eden, with large blossoms and leaves until Eve ate its forbidden fruit. As the tree's punishment for being an accomplice in her sin, its leaves shriveled to needles and its fruit changed into cones. Another legend claims the tree regained some of its original beauty when it bloomed again on the night of the Nativity and thus became the first Christmas tree.

Many ancient cultures celebrated the winter solstice with rituals involving trees, believing they symbolized life because they continued to grow even in the cold, dead of winter. The ancient Egyptians used date palms for their winter festival honoring Isis, the mother of their sun god, Horus, and the goddess of all growing things. Palm branches with twelve shoots represented the completion of the year and thus a victory of light over darkness.

The Romans used spruce and fir trees during their pagan

rituals to celebrate Saturnalia during the winter solstice. They decorated trees with lighted candles and trinkets honoring their sun god Saturn and paraded around with them in celebration of the gods who allowed the sun to return in the spring.

The oak tree has strong associations with the Christmas season. It was used not only for sacred rituals of ancient cultures, but it was also used as the popular Yule log. The oak has always symbolized strength, power and immortality. The Druids and Celts considered it especially sacred, and even the mistletoe that grew on it was considered holy because of its physical attachment to the tree. The Druids decorated the oak with gilded apples and lighted candles dedicated to their sun god. The Jews, Greeks and Romans also shared the belief that the oak was sacred.

The history of our modern-day Christmas tree originates in the eighth century in Germany. The Germans are credited with many of the traditions, history and popularity surrounding the Christmas tree. St. Boniface, a British monk and missionary in Germany, is credited as the person responsible for the first association of an evergreen tree, in this case a fir tree, as the Tree of the Christ Child. In 722, in a sermon to the Druids about the Nativity, he chopped down an oak tree to illustrate his point that the oak was neither sacred nor indestructible. They were horrified at this sacrilege. In the course of its fall, the oak destroyed everything in its path except a small fir tree. Proclaiming the fir's survival a miracle and thus giving it the same sacred and magical powers that he had just denounced, St. Boniface then honored it by declaring it the Tree of the Christ Child. Subsequent Christmas celebrations in Germany adopted the custom of planting fir saplings. In 1539, the Cathedral of Notre Dame in Strasborg displayed its first Christmas tree decorated with paper flowers, cookies, fruit and nuts.

In the Middle Ages, people set up "Paradise Trees" in their homes on Christmas Eve to symbolize the events of Adam and Eve in the Garden of Eden. According to the old Christian calendar, December 24 was the feast day of Adam and Eve. The popular miracle plays of that time were designed to educate the people about religion and theology. An evergreen tree was used as a stage prop to represent the tree of temptation in the Garden of Eden.

Because of its color, the evergreen was the logical choice during the drab winter season. It was decorated with apples to symbolize the forbidden fruit. People of that time liked to replicate these trees in their homes, sometimes adding small figures of Adam and Eve and the serpent under the tree. Later, flat wafers of cinnamon were also attached to symbolize the forgiveness of sins. Paper roses were affixed to the tree as well, to represent the Virgin Mary, thus covering the full span of Christianity, from the creation of the world to the gift of everlasting life.

Germany furthered its claim to the tradition of the modern-day Christmas tree through Martin Luther. One story concerning Luther states that while walking home one winter night, he was awed by the brilliant stars in the indigo winter sky against a background of evergreen trees. To teach others that Jesus was the "light of the world," he decided to place lighted candles on an evergreen as a symbol of the life-giving light and to replicate the beautiful winter scene that had inspired him.

The customs and traditions of the Christmas tree spread to the rest of Europe and England and from there to the American colonies. However, early Puritans were not enthusiastic about Christmas celebrations, decorations or gift-giving. In fact, a law enacted in 1659 in Massachusetts banned all frivolity and celebrations during the Christmas season, labeling them as distractions from the sacredness of the

Nativity: "Whosoever shall be found observing any such day as Christmas and the like, either by forbearing labor, feasting, or any other way upon such account as aforesaid, every such person so offending shall pay for each offense five shillings as a fine to the country." Fortunately, the law was repealed in 1681.

From these many and varied beginnings, the celebration of Christmas became popular in the United States around the beginning of the nineteenth century. People began to bring available greenery into their homes to provide color and decoration during the gray, dreary time of winter, much like their ancestors had years before. The millions of European immigrants who came to America brought their Christmas traditions with them from their old countries, and blended them with the customs of their new country.

For pioneer families, the cedar tree was the tree of choice for Christmas because of its ready abundance. Cedar

Christmas trees were common in homes, schools, churches and other public meeting places. In addition to the native blue berries on the tree, they were decorated with ornaments and the actual Christmas gifts for the family. Other decorations from the plant world adorned the tree, including popcorn and cranberry garlands. While warming log cabins and dugouts on cold winter nights, the cedar also served as a pioneer version of the traditional Yule log.

In 1856, Franklin Pierce became the first president to establish the tradition of having a Christmas tree in the White House. Each year, the National Christmas Tree Association sponsors a competition to select the perfect tree to serve as the national Christmas tree in the White House. Invitations are extended to artists, artisans and craftspeople to contribute decorations for the tree.

The fir and pine trees dominate as favorite Christmas trees, and each has its own special Christmas legend. In a popular legend about the fir tree, a cold and hungry child knocked at the door of a poor woodcutter one snowy Christmas Eve. Because the child was so small and lonely, in addition to being hungry and cold, the woodcutter's family welcomed him into their meager home and provided him with food and warmth both from the hearth and their hearts. On Christmas Day, the child appeared with a golden light surrounding him. The family recognized immediately that he was indeed the Christ Child. To repay their warmth and kindness, the Christ Child planted a tiny fir tree next to their door, with the promise that whenever the tree bore fruit, it would bring good fortune and blessings to the family. From that time on, the tree always bore fruit on Christmas Day.

The pine tree played a special role in providing shelter and protection for Joseph, Mary and Jesus during their flight into Egypt. Joseph noticed a tall pine tree with a hollow cavity in its trunk, almost like a small cave. The Holy Family tucked themselves into the hole, and the tree dropped its branches to hide them as Herod's armies chased by in pursuit. The tree hid them throughout the night. The following morning, the Christ Child blessed the tree with the gift of remaining green through all the seasons. The upturned branches and needles remind us to focus our thoughts and attitudes heavenward.

Although not used as decoration, frankincense and myrrh, two of the gifts to the Christ Child by the Wise Men, can also be considered Christmas trees. Frankincense is a gum resin obtained from the sap of the frankincense tree, found in Arabia and Africa. Myrrh is a fragrant, bitter-tasting gum resin also from several plants related to frankincense and is found in Arabia and east Africa. Frankincense and myrrh were especially meaningful gifts because in ancient times, they were used to make luxurious perfumes and incense, certainly worthy gifts for a king. Myrrh was also used to prepare bodies for burial. This gift foretold the death of Christ at his birth.

Although green is the most common color of Christmas, the type of greenery used varies from region to region of the present-day United States. People use readily available plants native to their region for Christmas trees and wreaths. Firs, spruce and pine are common in the northern climates, while jasmine and magnolia leaves are used in the south, and cactus is a common Christmas "tree" in the southwest. People in cotton producing areas often tuck tufts of cotton among the branches to create an illusion of snow in climates where flakes of snow seldom fall.

Wreaths
The Circle of Life

Wreaths have been used for centuries to signify the unending cycle of life. Historically, the wreath also symbolized victory and honor. A wreath formed of natural materials is all the more meaningful because it weaves nature into the spiritual circle of life—a circle with no beginning and no end.

The ancients believed that the leaves of plants and trees knew all the secrets of life, possibly a reference to the forbidden tree in the Garden of Eden. One legend tells the story of a magician who created a circle of leaves that he placed lightly on his head, just resting on his ears so he could listen to the secrets of the leaves as they whispered and rustled. He became wise and powerful, and others began to copy his idea so they could also learn the magic secrets of life. In time, it became the custom to crown a person with a wreath of leaves to recognize his great wisdom. Wreaths became the common man's crown, representing honor and wisdom in much the same way as the golden crowns of royalty represented their power, authority and honor.

We know that the ancient Romans, Druids and Celts used evergreen boughs and branches in their yearly Saturnalia and winter solstice celebrations, and probably began to create wreaths and circles from the boughs to conform with the wreaths they used for honor and victory. As early as 1444, documents tell of evergreen boughs being used as Christmas decorations in the streets of London. In sixteenth-century Germany, branches of fir or spruce were intertwined in a circular shape to symbolize the love of God, which has no beginning or end. The wreath was placed on a table and on each of the four Sundays of Advent, a lighted candle was attached to the wreath.

The Christmas legend about the origin of the Christmas wreath is very similar to the legends of the poinsettia and the Christmas rose. This legend tells of a young girl of Bethlehem who wept because she had nothing but a small wreath of holly leaves to bring to the Christ Child. Sadly, she offered her gift to the Child, and when she did, the leaves became shiny and glossy, and scarlet berries appeared where her tears had fallen.

A popular Christmas custom today is to create an

Advent wreath to use throughout the season in both churches and homes. The word "Advent" comes from the Latin word *Adventus* meaning "the coming" or "the arrival." Advent begins the Christian year on the liturgical calendar observed by the Roman Catholic Church and many Protestant churches, including United Methodist, Presbyterian, Episcopalian and Lutheran. Advent is a time of celebration, anticipation and preparation for the coming of the promised Messiah, with music and special worship services such as "Hanging of the Greens."

The Advent wreath is a Lutheran custom from eastern Germany that symbolizes God's eternal love and mercy through the circular form of the wreath. Green, the church's color for new life and hope, symbolizes the new life and hope that the birth of the Christ Child brings to the world. Four candles encircle a white candle, which is the Christ candle in the center. One candle is lit on each of the four Sundays preceding Christmas, and the center candle is lit on Christmas Eve.

The wreath is a symbol of the unending circle of life as evidenced in the life of Christ. The Advent wreath anticipates the Nativity while the crown of thorns, another form of a wreath, was worn at the Crucifixion. Although the crown of thorns was intended as a cruel insult to Jesus' preaching, it could instead symbolize the wisdom and honor of a common man whose life became a model and guide for all humankind.

The Yule Log

Although not a common custom in the United States, the burning of the Yule log is a common Christmas practice in many northern European countries. The warmth of the hearth aglow with the Yule log symbolizes the warmth and glow of the Christmas season.

Fire has always had a sacred meaning in man's attempts to communicate with the spirit world. The Celts and Teutons used fire in their winter festivals to celebrate the return of the sun. They built huge bonfires on the highest hills to honor their god, Odin. Young men often jumped over the bonfire to exhibit their courage.

The Yule log is believed to have originated in northern Europe with the Druids. During Saturnalia, they selected a large log from an oak tree, their favorite and most sacred tree. After blessing the log, they prayed for its power to burn eternally while watching diligently to assure that the log burned throughout the traditional twelve days of ceremony during the winter solstice.

Another legend derived from Druid history involves the mystical tree Yggdrasil, a tree so enormous that no man could even imagine its size. It was so large that it had three roots: one in heaven, one in hell and one on earth. The Druids believed that serpents were constantly gnawing at its roots and when they had finally gnawed through the roots completely, the universe would be destroyed.

When the Druids and other pagan tribes accepted Christianity, they had to reject their former rituals and symbols. In order to get the pagans to reject their beliefs, Christian leaders provided a substitute custom. Such was the case with the Yule log, which represented the ancient Yggdrasil. The burning of the log symbolized the destruction of this heathen belief and the acceptance of Christ as the light of the world.

The Vikings also used the Yule log as part of their winter celebrations. They carved runes into the wood representing undesirable traits, such as dishonor, and bad luck that they wanted the gods to take away from them. The burning of the log then symbolized the removal of these bad qualities.

Traditionally, the actual log that was to become the Yule log was selected months before the Christmas holidays in order for it to dry and season properly to assure that it would be long-burning. The log, also known as the "brand," was as large as the fireplace could accommodate and sizable enough to burn through the twelve traditional days of Christmas. Many times, the log still contained roots from the tree.

Bringing in the Yule log was a major family celebration involving all generations and even the household servants. It was believed that anyone who helped bring in the massive trophy would avoid any harm or injury from witchcraft in the coming year. The parade of celebrants sang joyful songs, played games and performed innocent tricks on each other during this festive time. As might be expected, many of the children liked to ride on the log as it was carried through the countryside and into the home.

Once inside, there were more traditions to honor the Yule log and to ensure good luck and good will in the coming year. Some of these traditions included sitting on the log, kissing it to receive its blessings, and pouring wine on the log three times while praying that health, wealth and happiness would come to everyone in the household. Usually, the oldest member of the family performed this ceremony. When the Yule log had been placed in the fireplace with all proper respect and honor, the remains of the previous year's log were brought out to use as kindling for the new log.

The Yule log was alleged to have special magical powers to protect the home from evil spirits and to heal misunderstandings and hatreds between people. The warm, glowing fire from the Yule log encouraged people to come together. The tables were loaded with all kinds of holiday foods, and games, stories, toasts, drinks and songs all created a spirit of harmony to end the old year and begin the new.

As the tradition of burning the Yule log spread, superstitions also abounded surrounding the do's, don'ts, and idiosyncrasies of its burning. The Yule log represented good luck and prosperity for the coming year, so many rituals accompanied its burning to ensure its beneficial results. Although varying from country to country, some of the most common traditions and superstitions included that only a person with freshly washed hands could touch the log; barefoot or squint-eyed persons entering the room with the burning log brought bad luck with them; and if the fire should happen to go out during the night, bad luck was a surety for the coming year. People often carried small pieces of the log to bed with them as protection against fire, lightning, thunder and witchcraft, which was believed to be especially potent during this time of the year.

Each year, a part of the log was saved to use as kindling for the next year's log. Even the ashes were valued as fertile amendments to the garden soil to make it more productive, and they were scattered on the branches of fruit trees to encourage fruiting. The ashes were also alleged to rid cats of vermin, to purify well water and to cure toothaches. In some places, they were placed under the bed as a protection from lightning. So with ashes under the bed, a piece of the Yule log tucked under the pillow, and a sprig of holly hung on the bedpost, a person was guaranteed pleasant dreams and protection from disaster and evil spirits.

The Holy Holly

Deck the halls with boughs of holly . . .

Since ancient times, holly has been considered a holy or sacred plant. The Druids and Romans used holly in their pagan rituals during the winter solstice because its green color symbolized eternal life. The traditional red and green colors of Christmas appear in the glossy, green leaves of the holly plant and in the vibrant, contrasting red berries. In religious symbolism, green signifies nature, youth and hope of eternal life. Red symbolizes fire, blood and charity. The holly plant brings together these contrasting images and symbols.

Holly and mistletoe, seasonal Christmas favorites, share many of the same traditions and legends. The Druids considered both holly and mistletoe symbols of eternal life because they remained green all year. They wore sprigs of holly in their hair when they gathered the sacred mistletoe during the special ceremonies of the winter solstice.

The Romans also celebrated the winter solstice during Saturnalia, a festival honoring their god, Saturn. Holly was the sacred plant of Saturn, and therefore, the Romans exchanged wreaths of holly and decorated their homes with it in his honor. They also believed the holly had special charms to ward off evil spells and lightning and that any plant that could survive winter would strengthen their homes. Along with being used for winter decorations, the Romans also planted it close to their homes.

Although holly was considered sacred to pagan gods, the early Christians began to use it in their Nativity celebrations as a ruse to conceal their Christianity. In this way, they appeared to be participating in Saturnalia festivities with the other Romans while they were actually celebrating the birth of Christ.

Because of its association with pagans, holly, like the mistletoe, was banned by the early Christian church, especially during Saturnalia. However, by the 1600s, the ban was lifted because the Christians began to associate holly with legends about its role in the crucifixion. One legend claims the holly sprang up beneath the footsteps of Christ on his way to the crucifixion, with the red berries representing his blood. Other legends claim that holly made up the crown of thorns that Christ wore on the cross, and the berries, which were originally white, became stained red when the sharp leaves pierced his skin. The wood of holly is hard and even-grained, and therefore excellent for construction. Unfortunately, it carries the stigma of being used for the crucifixion cross, a legend that it shares with mistletoe and the dogwood tree.

There are two types of holly — one genus grows sharp, prickly, pointed leaves (considered the masculine strain), and the other grows smooth, rounded leaves (considered the feminine line). According to European tradition, the first holly brought into the house during the Christmas season determined who would rule the house during the next year, the husband or the wife. Holly brought into a house before Christmas Eve would cause family quarrels. But on the other hand, people often settled disputes and quarrels under a holly tree because it symbolized peace and joy.

Charles Dickens made many references to holly, as well as mistletoe and ivy, in his seasonal favorite *A Christmas Carol*. Published in 1843, the book provides wonderful descriptions of country Christmas traditions of the time. Two of the ghosts in Ebeneezer Scrooge's dreams were adorned with holly: the Spirit of Christmas Past held a branch of fresh holly in its hand, and the Spirit of Christmas Present wore a holly wreath set with shining icicles.

In addition to its great popularity as a Christmas

decoration, holly has been attributed with having healing powers for dropsy, rheumatism, gout and asthma. Holly tea was brewed in parts of Germany, Russia and India, while Native Americans used the tea to treat measles. Birds like to dine on the red berries, but the bright, bead-like berries are poisonous to humans, inducing vomiting.

Holly planted near a house protected it from lightning, thunder, fire, witchcraft and, of course, the evil eye — the worst threat of all. Holly could also inflict disaster on a house if it was burned while green, if the berries were smashed, or if holly flowers were brought into the house during the summer. But a sprig of holly tucked on the bedpost is guaranteed to bring happy dreams, and holly decorations throughout the house create a jolly and joyful atmosphere. English poet George Wither describes it best in his sixteenth-century verse:

> *So now is come our joyfulest feast;*
> *Let every man be jolly.*
> *Each room with holly leaves is dressed*
> *And every post with holly.*

The Passionate Poinsettia

The red of the poinsettia is a passionate color, a vibrant, deep red. The legends of the poinsettia attest to this passion and intensity with stories of the fervor of young love and the rage inflamed by war.

Like other traditional Christmas plants and flowers, the poinsettia shares a pagan heritage but from a different part of the globe. The poinsettia, native to Mexico, was cultivated by the Aztecs for its brilliant red color which symbolized purity to them. It also had practical uses as a reddish-purple dye made from the bracts and as a medicine to reduce fever.

"Cuetlaxochitl" was the name used by the Aztecs to describe the flaming, red flower native to a place called

Cuetlaxochotlan, near present-day Taxco, Mexico. The indigenous name meant "flower which wilts," describing its natural tendency to fade quickly and have a short life span. The Aztecs had a special legend about how the poinsettia was created. It is a love story. A beautiful Aztec princess and warrior fell in love. As in many famous love stories, the two young lovers were unable to be together. The princess languished and died without the sustaining love of her warrior, much like a flower wilts without water and sunlight. Xoxhipilli, the flower goddess, changed her into the passionate, flaming red poinsettia to honor her chastity and purity.

The Toltecs, a contemporary, but enemy tribe to the Aztecs, also had a legend that described how the brilliant, red leaves of the poinsettia came to be. In a battle to defend the temple of their god Quetzalcoatl against the Aztecs, all the elder warriors were killed, leaving only the young boys of the tribe to continue the battle. The boys gathered the plumed headdresses of the slain warriors and put them on in an effort to disguise their youth. Quetzalcoatl looked down from the heavens and, inspired by the boys' courage against tremendous odds, transformed the feathers into living flames. When the Aztec warriors saw the temple surrounded by tongues of fire, they became terrified and retreated to their home tribes, leaving the remaining Toltecs in peace. When the children removed their headdresses and placed them on the ground, the beautiful poinsettia — the plant with leaves like living flames — sprang up around the temple as a tribute to their bravery and passion.

Later, when a group of Franciscan priests settled near Taxco in the 17th century, they adopted the poinsettia as part of their Nativity celebration because it naturally bloomed during the Advent season. It was a tradition for Mexican worshipers to bring flowers to place around the manger built at the church altar during the Nativity season.

Another Mexican tale involves a poor little girl who wanted very much to participate in this annual tradition of love and honor, but had no flowers or gift to place on the manger. So, sorrowfully and in tears, she walked to the church for the Christmas service. Suddenly, an angel appeared beside her and asked why she was crying. She answered that she had no gift to give to the Christ Child to show her love.

The angel told her to gather an armful of the weeds growing by the roadside and to place them on the manger. The little girl resisted the angel's suggestion because she felt embarrassed to place weeds among the beautiful flowers on the altar. However, the angel encouraged her to do as she said, promising that if she did, the Christ Child would know how true and sincere her love was for Him.

As the child placed her armful of weeds on the manger, they burst into the brilliant scarlet flowers of the poinsettia.

A miracle — again the power of passion and love! For that reason, the poinsettia is known as "La Flor de Nochebuena" or the "flower of the Holy Night."

The first poinsettias in the United States came as a gift from Joel Poinsett, the first U.S. Ambassador to Mexico from 1825 to 1829. He noticed the brilliant color of the plant during a visit to Taxco during the Christmas season and called it "the plant with the painted leaves." The petals of the plant are actually leaves or bracts. Because Poinsett was a botanist, he had some of the flowers sent to his plantation home in Greenville, South Carolina. The poinsettias thrived in his greenhouse, and he shared them with friends, spreading their popularity throughout the United States. Although the plant already had the Latin botanical name of *Euphorbia pulcherrima*, it became commonly known as the poinsettia, named for Ambassador Poinsett.

Rosemary, or the Rose of Mary

Are you going to Scarborough Fair?
Parsley, sage, rosemary, and thyme.

From biblical times and the Roman Empire to a folk song of the 1960s, rosemary has been a popular herb that appears in many myths, literature, customs and songs. The name "rosemary" suggests the plant might at one time have been known as the "rose of Mary," an allusion to the Virgin Mary. However, the name actually comes from the Latin word *rosmarinus*, meaning "dew of the sea," suggesting its native origin around the Mediterranean Sea.

Rosemary is an evergreen plant *(Rosemarinus offici-nalis)* belonging to the mint family. It blooms clusters of small, light blue flowers and grows leaves that yield a fragrant oil used in perfumes and cooking. Greek students often wore rosemary in their hair at exam time to assist their memories. Today, rosemary is most commonly recognized as a pungent herb used to season meats, vegetables and bread, and to scent potpourris and bath fragrances.

The Christmas history of the rosemary plant began with its association as a Christmas evergreen. During the Middle Ages, it was customary to spread rosemary on the floor at Christmas so that when people stepped on it, a pleasant pungent fragrance wafted through the house. Legend claims the plant received its gift of fragrance when

Mary placed the swaddling clothes of the Christ Child over it on the night of his birth. The rosemary bush also provided shelter for Mary during the Holy Family's flight into Egypt. When she threw her robe over the bush to create a hiding place, its white flowers changed into its familiar blue flowers, the color of her robe. Even today, it is a popular custom in Mediterranean villages to spread linens over rosemary bushes to dry and perfume them. Ancient stories also claim that rosemary grows upward for thirty-three years, matching the height of Jesus at his death. If the plant lives beyond thirty-three years, it only grows outward.

Rosemary has been a popular plant and decoration during the Christmas season for centuries, placed at the altar to attract special blessings and to guarantee protection against evil spirits. It has also been used to garnish the boar's head at Christmas feasts.

Rosemary was also a popular plant for love and romance customs, culminating with special traditions at wedding celebrations. In medieval times, young maidens slipped sprigs of rosemary under their pillows to attract their true love in their dreams. Ancient Romans considered it an aphrodisiac. A sprig of rosemary was tucked in bridal bouquets to symbolize happiness and was given by the bride to her new husband to ensure his fidelity to her. It was also added to the wedding cup shared by the wedding guests.

Anne of Cleves, the ill-fated wife of Henry VIII, wore rosemary in her crown at her wedding to the king, while Napoleon was so enamoured with the fragrance of rosemary that legends claim he used over one hundred bottles of rosemary water on his honeymoon.

The pungent and poetic rosemary is a plant that honors both beginnings and endings. Funeral mourners carried sprigs of rosemary as tokens of remembrance for the deceased and later planted it near the grave as a promise of eternal faithfulness. Shakespeare's immortal lines in *Hamlet* remind us to honor rosemary as a symbol of eternal remembrance:

There's rosemary, that's for remembrance
pray love, remember . . .

The Christmas Rose

Is a rose always a rose?

The flower known as the Christmas Rose actually isn't part of the rose family at all, but is related to the buttercup, the flowers that legends tell us are the stars that fell from the heavens on the night of Christ's birth.

The Christmas Rose, like the holly, also shared condemnation by early church leaders because of its association with Roman immorality and debauchery. The Romans and Greeks had dedicated the rose to the goddess of love and the god of war. With such associations, there was no way that it could be allowed to symbolize the Virgin Mary and her purity in church settings.

The original home of the Christmas Rose *(Helleborus Niger)* was Egypt. From there, it was taken to Greece where it picked up its name Helleboros, meaning "plant eaten by fawns." The Christmas Rose is a winter blooming plant with blossoms similar to a buttercup, but in a variety of colors. The petals were often strewn through the house to guard against evil spirits. The rhizomes are poisonous but have been used as a heart stimulant and cathartic as well as for treatment of epilepsy, gout and mental disorders.

The Christmas Rose shares a story similar to those of the poinsettia and the wreath. This legend redeemed the flower from its lusty past and restored honor to it. In this version, it was a shepherd girl who could offer no gift to the Christ Child. She was deeply saddened as she watched the Wise Men arrive with their rich, exotic gifts and as the shepherds presented their humbler gifts. Realizing she had nothing of any value to give, she began to cry. An angel saw her misery, and using a lily as a magic wand, transformed the child's tears into the white petals tinged with pink of the Christmas Rose. The plant burst into blossom for the first time ever, and the girl gathered an armful to present to the Baby. She was over-joyed when he reached out for her flowers instead of the gifts of the Magi.

Modern day folklore advises that the Christmas Rose should be planted by the door to welcome Christ into the home. The Christmas Rose is also known as the Flower of St. Agnes, the patroness of purity who became a martyr at age thirteen for professing her faith in 300 A.D. She is honored on her feast day, January 21.

Mmmm . . . Cinnamon

The sweet, but tangy scent of cinnamon flavors the Christmas kitchen and invites us into the warmth and wonder of the season. Cinnamon is a spice that leaves its signature flavor not only on our taste buds, but also in our memory, blending nostalgic recollections of past Christmases with delightful anticipation of the tastes and treats of the present Christmas.

Cinnamon is native to India and Sri Lanka and is easily grown in hot, humid, tropical climates. If left untended, the cinnamon tree will grow to a height of 30 to 50 feet. However, for cultivation purposes, the shoots of the tree are trimmed twice each year. The yellowish-brown outer bark is scraped off to expose pale, brown strips of inner bark. As it dries, the bark curls itself into quills. The thinnest quills are the most highly desired.

Ground cinnamon is popular in pastries, breads, cookies and puddings — all those delectable Christmas goodies and treats. Stick cinnamon is used in preserved fruit, pickles, soups and beverages, especially hot cider, tea, and cocoa — perfect complements to Christmas cookies and cakes. It is often used as a decoration on wreaths and centerpieces. Oil of cinnamon is distilled from the bark and used for medicinal purposes and flavoring.

Long before the time of Christ, spices were highly valued throughout Old Testament lands and Asia. The Babylonians and Indians were trading partners 4500 years ago, and the Chinese were spice traders dealing in cinnamon, pepper and cloves over 3000 years ago. Throughout history, cinnamon has been a valued spice, both as a trading commodity and as a flavor enhancer.

The Old Testament makes frequent reference to spices and traders in its stories, including the sale of Joseph by his brothers to a caravan of Ishmaelite spice traders, the anointing oils for the dead, and the use of incense to be burned in the temples. It is probable that cinnamon was one of the spices traded. The Queen of Sheba visited King Solomon with a great caravan of camels loaded with gold, gems, and spices including cinnamon. The king declared that her gift of cinnamon was a prized part of his treasury.

Flavor enhancement was only one of the many uses of cinnamon. The prized bark also had medicinal value and was an ingredient for love potions, perfume and incense, especially by the rich upper classes. It is said that over one year's supply of cinnamon was burned at Nero's funeral in Rome.

Because of their strategic location, the Arabs had a

monopoly on cinnamon and other highly desired spices until the first century A.D. To protect their treasure and to discourage any competitors, they created a shrewd story as rich and spicy as many of the recipes that contained the flavorful spice. The Arabs claimed that cinnamon grew on a huge tree in the center of a lake guarded by large vulture-like birds that were as fierce as dragons. The bravest traders would risk their lives to gather the cinnamon by luring the beasts away from the tree with chunks of raw meat. While the beasts were distracted, others would swim through the murky, marshy waters to break off as many branches as they could carry.

Another version told by Herodotus, a Greek historian and traveler, told of dangerous eagles that made their nests of cinnamon sticks. In this story, the brave traders also lured the birds away with raw meat. When they flew back to their nests with the meat, the extra weight was so great that pieces of the cinnamon nest would break off, and the traders would rush in to collect them. Of course, such daring feats and risks commanded high prices for cinnamon, as well as helped the Arabs remain the sole source of the popular spice.

Much of the cinnamon came by way of Malaysia and Indonesia to Madagascar, a 4500-mile journey by sea in double outrigger canoes. From there, it was carried up the coast of east Africa to the Red Sea. The journey of cinnamon from its source in Malaysia and Indonesia was long, arduous and dangerous. The threat of spice thieves and dragon-like eagles made the spice even more desirable, exotic and expensive.

From these exotic trade routes, cinnamon has made its way into our Christmas recipes and decorations, sprinkling its flavor and aroma into our sensory memories of Christmas traditions.

Peppermint

. . . and leave a peppermint stick
for old St. Nick
hanging on the Christmas tree.

Peppermint, as its name suggests, is a member of the mint family. The mint botanical family tree is made up of up to 6,000 different species. Legend claims peppermint can provide relief from stomach disorders and indigestion, chapped hands, and mouth and gum sores. If rubbed on a table, it will create an appetite in whoever sits there, but it can also be used to repel mice and other rodents. Peppermint is very similar to hyssop, which is also a member of the mint family and was used in Old Testament times for ceremonies of purification and sacrifice. The mint family is native to the Mediterranean region and central Asia. Plants in this family are usually low shrubs with aromatic, perfumed leaves.

The peppermint candy cane, whose flavoring is derived from the peppermint plant, is a universal symbol of Christmas. Its history and legend date back almost as far as the decorated Christmas trees in Europe. Its shape of a cane represents exactly that — the crook of the ancient shepherd's cane, used to rescue or grab errant sheep. Through the years, it has become a Christmas symbol to honor the humble shepherds who were the first visitors to the manger.

Plain white-sugar candy sticks were popular in the 1700s when people used common items, especially food and candy, to decorate their Christmas trees. They were also popular treats for children, often used to quiet restless children during the long, traditional Christmas church services or as pacifiers for fussy babies. One legend says that the choirmaster of the Cologne Cathedral persuaded the local confectioners to bend the ends of the traditional white candy stick to represent shepherd's crooks. He then distributed them to the children so they would behave well during the services. From Cologne, the custom of handing out candy canes became popular throughout Europe. Often these canes were adorned with sugar roses.

The candy cane arrived in the United States with the European immigrants. In 1847, a German-Swedish immigrant, August Imgard of Wooster, Ohio, used candy canes and paper ornaments to decorate a blue spruce tree for his nieces and nephews to commemorate the customs of his homeland.

The red and white stripes and peppermint flavoring weren't added until the turn of the century. The McCormack family of Albany Georgia played an important role in promoting the familiar red and white candy. In the 1920s, Bob McCormack began making candy canes as special Christmas treats for his children, family and friends. At that time, the entire process was done by hand and was very time consuming and labor intensive, which limited the distribution to only a few close friends and family. It was not until the 1950s that the process was made easier when Gregory Keller, a Catholic priest and brother-in-law to McCormack, invented a machine to mass-produce the candy. Younger generations of the McCormack family later developed a special package that allowed the delicate, fragile candy symbols to be transported beyond the local community.

Folklore attributes special symbolism to the candy beyond the shepherd's crook or the letter "J" for Jesus. The traditional colors of red and white have religious significance with the white representing the purity of Christ and the red his blood. The stripes are said to represent the beating endured by Jesus from Roman soldiers. While such symbolism is always subject to skepticism and criticism, these legends help create the aura, mystery and magic that make up the Christmas season.

. . . And Don't Forget the Cranberries

While many Christmas plants and flowers are celebrated in song and verse, the cranberry's value and beauty is celebrated in the poetry of recipes. In fact, there are more than 700 cranberry food products that could cover an entire gourmet smorgasbord from soup to dessert! The cranberry doesn't have the romantic history and religious folklore of the mistletoe, poinsettia, holly, and the many varieties of Christmas trees; rather, its history is one of function and utility.

The cranberry is a truly unique plant among the

traditional Christmas plants. It is one that we in the United States can call our own — a plant native and unique to the United States. The cranberry (*vaccinium macrocarpon*) is one of only three fruits native to North America, the other two being the Concord grape and the blueberry. Cranberries grow wild in boggy places from Newfoundland, western Ontario, and the northeastern and north central states as far south as North Carolina, Virginia, Ohio, Illinois, and Arkansas.

The cranberry shares its history with its native country. Native American tribes had already discovered its food, medicinal and decorative values long before the Europeans arrived. Two Native American legends tell of the unusual circumstances that caused the cranberry to grow in North America.

One legend of the cranberry dates back to prehistoric

times and comes from the Paleo-Indians, who were probably the first settlers in North America, arriving from Asia over the Bering Strait land bridge. The Paleo-Indians, known as The People, lived peacefully for many years with large, woolly, elephant-like animals, probably either mastodons or mammoths. They called them Yah-qua-whee. The Yah-qua-whee were much like the buffalo were to the Plains Indians, providing hides for clothing and shelter, meat for food, and bones for beads, tent frames, utensils and musical instruments.

Eventually the Yah-qua-whee rebelled against The People, destroying their homes and hurting and killing them, along with the smaller animals of the forest. The smaller animals and The People banded together to stop the rampaging Yah-qua-whee by digging huge pits and covering them with green branches as camouflage. They then drove the Yah-qua-whee to the pits with huge torches of fire. As a result of the struggle between The People and the smaller animals against the huge animals, the trampled ground became soft, soggy and bloody, and turned into huge bogs where many of the Yah-qua-whee, The People, and the smaller animals sank and died.

The survivors felt a great loss. Their family and friends were gone, and so were the companionship and services of their former friends the Yah-qua-whee. To ease their sorrow, the following spring, the Great Spirit caused the bloody bogs to come alive with delicate pink blossoms which turned into the bright, blood-red, bitter berries in the fall. The People learned to mix the berries with dried deer meat and fat to make pemmican for food and to create poultices and dyes from the berries. The cranberries were distributed at tribal feasts as a symbol of peace and the Great Spirit's abiding love and compassion for The People.

A different legend explains how the cranberry came to Cape Cod, one of the most prolific production areas in the United States. There was an argument between a Christian missionary and an Indian medicine man over an unknown topic. Although the missionary had been a long-time friend, the Indian cast a spell on him in a fit of anger, and caused the missionary to sink into a bog of quicksand. The two men agreed to settle their dispute in a contest of wits, which continued for over two weeks. Throughout the contest, a white dove flew to the missionary, placing a bright, red berry in his mouth to provide him with juice and food during this ordeal.

The Indian tried to shoo away the dove with all his tricks, charms and spells, but to no avail. Finally, completely exhausted, the Indian fell to the ground, the spell was broken and the missionary was set free. However, one red berry had dropped into the bog where it began to grow, creating the famous cranberry bogs in Cape Cod.

The Pilgrims received the cranberry as a friendship gift from the Wampanoag Indians who called it "ibimi," meaning bitter berry. The Plymouth colonists changed the name to "crane berries" because the vine's pink flowers with long stems resembled cranes. Crane berry was also easier for their British tongues to pronounce.

Historians still debate whether cranberries were part of the first Thanksgiving feast in 1621. Nonetheless, they became a popular food with the British colonists. British ships also carried cranberries as a preventive for scurvy. Cranberries were a popular, early export item to England where they brought premium prices in London. They were also sent as a token peace offering to Charles II in 1677 to help mollify his anger over the colonists minting their own coins.

Always resourceful, both the Indians and the settlers found many uses for the fruit and the leaves. A dye from the berries was used for cloth; a diuretic tea was made from the leaves; poultices came from the berries; and an astringent was used to stop bleeding. Cranberry juice is still recommended as a popular remedy for urinary tract ailments.

During Christmas, people began to use cranberries to decorate their trees, interspersing the berries like beads with popped popcorn on strings to create garlands to loop among the branches. This pioneer craft has made a comeback as modern families turn back to nature to create more traditional and natural decorations. Popcorn and cranberry strings often decorate outdoor Christmas trees to provide a midwinter's gourmet treat for birds and other wildlife.

Bibliography

Barth, Edna. *Holly, Reindeer, and Colored Lights*. New York: The Seabury Press, 1971.

Benning, Hayward. "Plants of the Winter Solstice." *Conservationist*. 1993, Vol. 48, no. 2, p. 30-34.

Borland, Hal. *Plants of Christmas*. New York: Thomas Y. Crowell, 1969, 1987.

"Candy Canes." http://www.snopes.com/holidays/xmas/cndycane.html.

"The Christmas Tree Legends." http://w/.igloo.com/info/santa/sec2-4html.

Conner, Ruth. "Holly for a Long Winter's Night." *Country Living*. Dec. 1989, Vol. 12, no. 12, p. 80.

Cooper, Elizabeth K. *And Everything Nice*. New York: Harcourt, Brace, and World, 1966.

"Cranberries Flow from Red Sea to Festive Table." *Daily Oklahoman*. November 28, 1997, p. 18.

Dowden, Anne Ophelia. *This Noble Harvest*. New York: William Collins Publishers, 1979.

Dreany, Joseph. *The Magic of Spices*. New York: G.P. Putnam's Sons, 1961.

Gemming, Elizabeth. *The Cranberry Book*. New York: Coward - McCann, Inc., 1983.

Graham-Barber, Lynda. *Ho, Ho, Ho! The Complete Book of Christmas Words*. New York: Bradbury Press.

Greene, Ellin. *The Legend of the Cranberry: A Paleo-Indian Tale*. New York: Simon & Schuster Books for Young Readers, 1993.

Hottes, Alfred C. *Garden Fact and Fancies*. New York: Dodd, Mead, and Company, 1949, p. 293.

Howe, Maggy, "Mistletoe." *Country Living*. December 1995, Volume 18, no. 12, p. 54-57.

Krythe, Maymie. *All About Christmas*. New York: Harper & Row, 1954.

Muir, Frank. *Christmas Customs and Traditions*. New York: Taplinger Publishing Co., 1975.

Metcalfe, Edna. *The Trees of Christmas*. Nashville: Abington Press, 1969.

Murphy, G. Ronald. "Yggdrasil, The Cross and The Christmas Tree." *America*. Dec. 14, 1996, p. 16-20.

"Record Cranberry Crop is Predicted." *Stillwater NewsPress*. October 13, 1997, p. B8.

Reid, E. "The Poinsettia," *Bueno*. Winter, 1996, Vol. 6, no. 2, p. 11.

Sanders, Dori. "Aunt Vestula's Christmas Touches." *Southern Living*. December 1996, p. 194.

Snyder, Phillip V. *The Christmas Tree Book*. 1976.

"The Story of the Candy Cane."
http://www.bobscandies.com/symbolism.html.

Tuleja, Ted. *Curious Customs*. New York: Harmony Books, 1987.

Wexler, Mark. "Crimson Harvest." *Modern Maturity*. Vol. 38, no. 6, p. 58.